陽

365

Steps toward Harmony
Feng Shui

365 Steps toward Harmony – Feng Shui

Copy Editing: A-P-E, Overath
Cover design: BOROS, Wuppertal

© 2000 DuMont Buchverlag, Köln
(Dumont monte UK, London)

ISBN 3-7701-7024-5
Printed in Slovenia

1

Our quest for wisdom

bestows us with daily gains.
(Lao Zi)

2

Feng Shui

The Chinese word *feng* means "wind," *shui* means "water." (spoken
foong shwiy in Cantonese/*fung shoy* in Mandarine).

Together, they denote the dynamic and formative effects of wind
and water, their opposition, and the harmonic collaboration of
both elements.

3 Introduction and Application

Feng Shui is the Taoist teaching of how to live in harmony with nature and one's surroundings. For centuries the Chinese have relied on the practical wisdom of these teachings when choosing burial sites, locating and designing the interior of their homes, and especially in trying to construct daily life more harmoniously. This wisdom has been recorded in the *Book of Changes* (*I Ching*).

This Chinese tradition reached Europe in the 19th century. People damaged by civilisation and our hectic world have lost their intuition for finding the natural rhythm of life. Feng Shui offers a coherent system of advice for mastering daily life and improving general well being. The atmosphere of our surroundings affects our health. Practical Feng Shui can help us be more aware of and positively shape our surroundings. Its main aims are improving our lifestyle and health, creating a harmonious family life, and enjoying success in our work.

4

Qi

A central concept of Feng Shui is Qi (also written Chi or Ch'i).

Its meaning is best defined as "physiological activity," "the functional vitality of organisms," "life energy" or "life breath," or "active energy that flows through all things."

5

Everything flows like water,

without barriers: day and night.
(Kungtse, Lun yu, IX, 17)

Everything is constantly in motion, everything has its own energy field and everything is connected in some way. It is easier to follow the stream of Qi and to know what it favours, than to swim against the current. We should therefore be aware of the most important forms of Qi.

Every body, every form of existence has its own energy field.

6 In the human body this flows along the acupuncture points. Energy circulates in a field of growing plants. Wind and water carry energy with them, but even non-living things have their own energy fields. All energy fields directly influence each other, whether harmoniously, or strengthening or weakening each other— everything flows.

The natural, balanced flow of Qi should be respected. Seldom do we happen upon the perfect situation, but improving someone else's energy field positively affects our own. Feng Shui teaches you how to intervene to correct and strengthen, or tie together and channel, the flow of energy. Impediments can be removed, or at least reduced. The harmonious flow of Qi promotes health, affluence and the psyche, and creates a pleasant atmosphere.

7

One guideline maintains that Qi flowing in a straight line, for instance through an open front door along a straight hallway to a back door, creates energy that is too forceful and does not stay in the room. Circulating Qi is ideal, as it has a stimulating effect.

8

Planetary Qi

The constellation of the sun, zodiac signs and the force of the moon influence our lives. Specific stellar constellations cause people and animals alike to act strangely. Birds of passage will set off on their long voyages, high and low tides flow with the waning and growing of the moon, and so on. Pay attention to the lunar cycle and to your horoscope.

9

Atmospheric Qi

Electronic devices, synthetic materials, energy-efficient windows, air conditioning and heating, etc. have changed the "climate" in our surroundings. Qi is trapped in rooms and either flows away too quickly or cannot escape at all. Previously, slits and holes made even air circulation possible. Plants, landscape views and fountains can help linder this, but a regular exchange of air in rooms remains important. A pinwheel or wind chimes can indicate whether Qi is flowing.

10 Animal Qi

Animals are able to sense and give us an indication of where too much or too little Qi is flowing. The Qi surrounding them can have a positive effect on us. The sight of a tortoise is calming, for example, and goldfish in an aquarium have a positive effect on the atmosphere of a room.

11 Climatic Qi

The weather greatly affects our well being and characterises people living in a certain region. In dark, cold regions, for instance, people tend to move more slowly, repress their emotions and tend toward depression; whereas in sunny regions people are more expressive, active and effusive.

12

The Qi of Predecessors

Before moving into a building it is important to find out how the previous owner or tenant felt there. Many tenancy changes over a short space of time are ground for caution; ask about the reasons for the move so you can counteract them appropriately.

13

The Qi of Light

Light is instrumental for all life. It is also important for the flow of Qi, which can only flow effectively in a well lit room. This does not mean, however, that brightly lit spaces are beneficial to Qi; they can even hinder its energy. Areas in which perception is not restricted, where shadows cannot form, and where there is no blindingly bright light will help Qi develop. Artificial light should be avoided during the day. Blinds can keep out excessive light.

14

Warming Qi

Unlike light, warming Qi does not expand in a linear fashion. It spreads from a heat source in the room or is propelled into the room by a central furnace, for example. The principle remains the same, however: heat rises. For an even distribution one should avoid permanent drafts.

15

The Qi of the Road

Roads and paths are symbolic for the constant movement of humankind. They are comparable to the flow of a river. In choosing the site for your home, make sure that the flow does not bring any "pollution" into the house. A street should never pass directly by the front door. Never buy a house situated on a curve, unless it is on the inside of the curve, where there is less danger of collisions and accidents. Regarding the drainage system, one should ensure that clean water is transported into the house and refuse water away from the house.

16

According to Legend,

the roots of Feng Shui lie in the *Ho Shu*, the writings of the Yellow River.
Fu Xi, a scholar and the first ruler of China, is said to have been
meditating next to the Yellow River when a tortoise crept onto the bank.
Fu Xi observed the spiritual being representative of the universe, and
noticed the special pattern of its shell. In this, he recognised a scheme
according to which the five transubstantiatory elements (Earth, Fire,
Wood, Metal and Water) were represented by odd and even numbers.

17

In a simplified representation this scheme appears as a magical square, in which the sum of any line equals the number 15.

4	9	2
3	5	7
8	1	6

In *Luo Shu*, the writings of the River Luo, this magical square, related to the eight trigrams from the *Book of Changes*, forms the basis of the Ba-Gua (Ba = eight; Gua = trigram).

18

19

The Ba-Gua is an important aid to Feng Shui. It is a grid that can be laid over blueprints or floorplans in order to determine how different aspects of the inhabitants' lives correspond to the plans.

wood

south

earth

4　　　9　　　2

wood

east　3　　　5　　　7　autumn

west

spring

metal

8　　　1　　　6

earth

north

metal

The trigrams are eight pictures, each comprised of three lines. They are combined with each other to create the 64 pictures that are the basis for the life wisdom in the *Book of Changes* (*I Ching*). Each trigram corresponds to an element, a season, a direction, a number, etc.

20

KAN–Water

21

坎

Corresponds to:
the element Water, direction north, number one, season winter and the colours blue and black.

It represents the river of life and career, and is associated with danger.

KUN–Earth

22

坤

Corresponds to:
the element Earth, direction south-west, number two and the colour yellow.

It stands for dedication, unification and relationships, and is associated with motherliness.

23 ‒ ‒ CHEN–Thunder

Corresponds to:
the element Wood, direction east, number
three, season spring and the colour green.

It represents health, vitality, ancestors
and family, and is associated with movement
and new beginnings.

震

☴ SUN–Wind 24

Corresponds to:
the element Wood, direction southeast, number four and the colour green.

It represents prosperity, blessings and
growth, and is associated with wind and
intrusion.

巽

≡ **QIEN–Sky**

25

Corresponds to:
the element hard Metal, direction northwest,
number six and the colour gold.

It stands for leaders, mentors and
teachers, and is associated with strength
and domestic leadership.

⚏ **TUI–Lake**

26

Corresponds to:
the element soft Metal, direction west,
number seven, season autumn and the
colour gold.

It represents creativity, joy and children,
and is associated with merriment.

 **KEN–Mountain**

27

Corresponds to:
the element Earth, direction northeast,
number eight and the colour yellow.

It stands for insight and wisdom, and is
associated with peacefulness.

28

LI–Fire

Corresponds to:
the element Fire, direction south, number
nine, season summer and the colour red.

It stands for self-knowledge, the respect of
others and fame, and is associated with
cheerfulness.

The number five is at the centre of the Ba-Gua.

As a female character it is represented by the trigram KUN, and as a male character by the trigram KEN.

It is also frequently depicted as Yin and Yang, the energetic focal point and symbol of perpetual change.

29

30

Yin Yang

A circle parted by an s-shaped line, one half black (Yin, feminine or negative principle of nature), the other half white (Yang, male or positive principle of nature), symbolises the harmonious equilibrium between the rivalling forces of the universe. One cannot exist without the other, and inequalities should not be allowed to develop. The interplay of aspects of both principles yields a harmonious whole.

Specific characteristics are assigned to the principles of Yin and Yang:

Yin	**Yang**
female	male
dark	bright
shade	light
night	day
moon	sun
loose	firm
earth	sky
winter	summer
cool	warm
under	over
stillness	movement
passive	active
gentle	rough
sad	cheerful

32

The two schools of Feng Shui practice

The best-known directions of practice are the compass school, and the landscape or form school.

The compass school is very precise and works with concrete data, such as one's date of birth or zodiac sign. As the name reveals, a Feng Shui compass is a necessary tool.

The older landscape school is very logical, and can be understood with common sense.

The Compass School

The so-called Luo Ban compass (*Luo* = all; *Ban* = dish or disk) shows in what relation a person stands to the original source of the universe. Using the correct orientation, buildings or the furnishings of a room can be structured in a way similar to the heavenly constellations.

The Luo Ban compass is divided into concentric circles (as many as 38, but at least 4 rings) and 24 points. Each ring allows the calculation of one aspect of Feng Shui. In contrast to a western compass, it is oriented toward the south.

33

34

The Landscape School

Natural geological formations and, in a figurative sense, artificially created forms such as houses, roads or furniture have a certain effect on people living in the vicinity.

Land formations such as mountain peaks or river valleys, for example, are associated with animals who, in turn, symbolise particular characteristics and thus affect their surroundings. If plants grow better in certain locations, a healthy Qi is almost certainly at work. Geomancy helps us recognise advantageous and disadvantageous characteristics in the landscape.

Buildings should complement the landscape, rather than harming its appearance.

35

An ideal landscape is characterised by the togetherness of the Yang of mountaintops and the Yin of the plains. Steep mountain summits alone are oppressive, while a sterile, flat plain is not only monotonous and dreary, it is also unable to generate Qi.

36

Example 1: The Rice Bowl

The landscape school provides very graphic assistance.

A rock formation that looks like a rice bowl holds the promise of constant and sufficient provisions for people living nearby, even prosperity.

37

Example 2: The Needle

A rock jutting steeply and straight as a needle
toward the sky indicates learnedness. For the
people who are lucky enough to be living nearby,
it is a guarantee of growing
knowledge, progress in
research, and academic
success.

38

Example 3: The Head

Rocks can also be formed like heads. Chinese geomancy teaches that they act as guardians, protecting the surrounding houses. Associate freely and form your own conclusions about landscape formations!

39
Heavenly Creatures

The numerical pattern of the magical square is also related to the heavenly creatures.

Feng Shui practice designates one of the four heavenly creatures to each side of every property: the back of a house is guarded by the black tortoises, the facade by the red phoenix, the left side by the green dragon and the right side by the white tiger.

40

The luck-bringing tortoise with its powerful shell offers protection in the north. Its element is Earth.

The view ahead, toward the south, should not be impeded. Here the legendary phoenix watches over the property and keeps an eye on the surroundings. Its element is Fire.

41

42

The dragon is a god-like animal. It guards over the inhabitants from the left flank of the house, in the east, fulfilling all their wishes.

43

To the west, or the right, the tiger moves stealthily along the side of the property. It is seen as being dangerous and represents strength. Its element is Metal, and it keeps demons at bay.

The Five Elements

The world consists of materials that belong to one of the five elements: Water, Wood, Fire, Earth and Metal. Humans are in constant contact with these elements. They are to be seen not only as substances, but also as symbols of the characteristics of each element. Each corresponds to different activities, seasons, colours, shapes and directions. The effects of the individual elements on each other determine their particular development as well as the influence they have on their surroundings.

45

Practical Application

An investigation into the interaction of the elements makes it possible to analyse and improve someone's Qi, their personal development and their surroundings. For a positive Feng Shui it is necessary to know the course of the cycles and the elements and their meaning, whether for the interior design of rooms or buildings, when choosing a partner, or in many other situations.

Test which elements enhance each other in a given situation, which interact neutrally or completely counteract each other: Does the same element occur more than once? Try to avoid this or introduce a "destructive" element to maintain balance.

To strengthen one area, for example, knowledge of the element Earth, choose a "Fire" object, perhaps something red, in your working environment.

46

Wood

This element represents all living things: the plant world, spring, growth, activity, power, the east and rising energy.

High-rising, angular shapes are typical of the Wood element. It corresponds to the principles of Yang.

Fire

The element Fire represents expansion and is the ultimate measure of energy, burning, light, warmth, summer and the south.

Sharp, triangular shapes are associated with this Yang element.

Earth

The element Earth symbolises the Centre: the energy is staid and perfect, and is associated with the transition from one season to the next. Stability, safety and security are the corresponding characteristics; flat rectangles or cubes are the corresponding shapes. The preferred directions are the centre, southwest and northeast. Yin and Yang stand in equal proportion to each other.

48

Metal

The element Metal stands for maturity, return and stability, autumn and harvest time, and internally directed Yin energy. Round or semi-circular shapes belong to this element.

Water

Water includes everything that flows, from fog to the oceans. Its characteristics are winter, north, and irregular shapes. Water is a symbol for dissolving Yin energy.

51

Corresponding characteristics and objects that allow comprehensive interpretation:

Water	Wood	Fire	Earth	Metal
black/blue	green	red	yellow	white
waterworks	plant	candle	statue	clock
aquarium	chair	pyramid	clay pot	crystal
glass	music	horse	dog	chicken
north	east	south	centre	west
cold	wind	heat	wet	dry
fear	anger	joy	rationality	love

52

Each element corresponds to a specific area of the Ba-Gua:

Career	Water
Relationships	Earth
Ancestors/Family	Wood
Prosperity	Wood
Health	Earth
Patrons	Metal
Children	Metal
Knowledge	Earth
Fame	Fire

The Productive Cycle

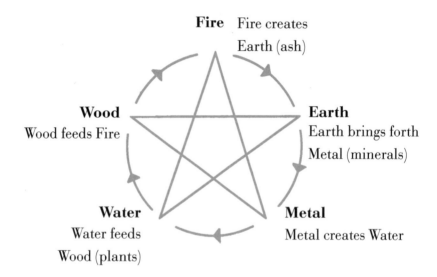

Fire   Fire creates Earth (ash)

Earth
Earth brings forth Metal (minerals)

Metal
Metal creates Water

Water
Water feeds Wood (plants)

Wood
Wood feeds Fire

54

The Destructive Cycle

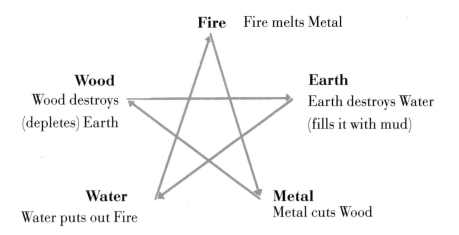

Fire Fire melts Metal

Wood
Wood destroys
(depletes) Earth

Earth
Earth destroys Water
(fills it with mud)

Water
Water puts out Fire

Metal
Metal cuts Wood

The Weakening Cycle

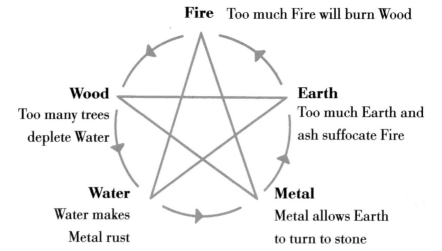

Fire   Too much Fire will burn Wood

Wood
Too many trees
deplete Water

Earth
Too much Earth and
ash suffocate Fire

Water
Water makes
Metal rust

Metal
Metal allows Earth
to turn to stone

**Everything
in the world changes,
nothing remains the same.**

(Zhuang Zi)

57

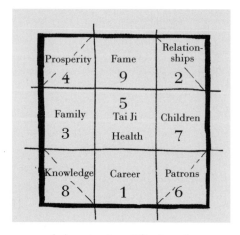

Prosperity 4	Fame 9	Relationships 2
Family 3	5 Tai Ji Health	Children 7
Knowledge 8	Career 1	Patrons 6

The Ba-Gua scheme is actually octagonal, but is simplified and presented as a square. Each of the eight outer fields represents a trigram that, in turn, is related to a certain aspect of our life. By applying this scheme to our homes or other spaces, we can ascertain which rooms correspond to which areas of our lives, and even come to certain realisations about the state of affairs in those areas.

In the middle is the Centre, or the area of Health, which sends its Qi into all the other areas.

58

The Ba-Gua plan can be applied to an entire piece of property, the yard, a house or individual rooms. Keep in mind that number 1, corresponding to Career, always points toward the north and number 9, the area of Fame, lies to the south.

1–Career

This field will tell you something about yourself, your life path and self-appraisal. How near or far away from your goals are you,

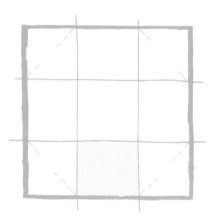

both in your career and in your private life? The Ba-Gua can also reveal something about your ability to negotiate business matters and your position in society. It is wise to design this area so that it flows and is supple.

2–Relationships

All your relations to others are mirrored in this area: your relationship with your partner, with colleagues, business partners and neighbours. If this area is cluttered, or one where plants die rather than thrive, you should immediately devote some additional attention to your interpersonal contacts.

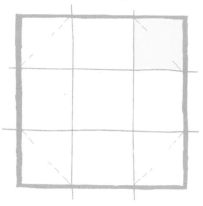

3–Ancestors/Family

This field deals with the past, roots, ancestors and your relationship with your parents. Difficulties and impediments here denote that you should clarify any unsettled relationships with your family members as quickly as possible.

62

4–Prosperity

This area tells you about your ability to create and maintain both spiritual and substantive wealth.

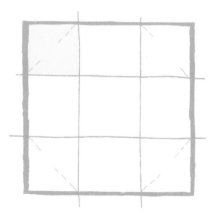

5–Health/Centre

Well being and vitality emanate from the Centre to all the other areas. The more effectively energy is collected here, without its flow being impeded, the more positive its effects on the other areas of your life will be.

6–Patrons

According to Chinese tradition, this field is dedicated to spirits and deities, and represents all those who protect, help and support us in our times of need.

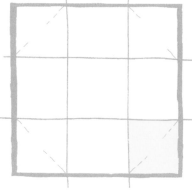

65

7–Children

Creativity and activity are reflected in this area, including hobbies and the effective use of free time. If you have the feeling that you are uncreative and lack ideas you should change something in this area. This field also gives us insight into our relationship with children in general.

8–Knowledge

Education and intuition are equally represented here. How open are you to change? How do you react to it? Create a space for contemplation and meditation in this area and take a break from your daily routine!

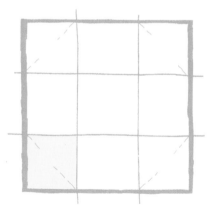

9–Fame

This area shows what standing you enjoy, both in public and among
your friends. The way you are perceived obviously depends on your inner
maturity and charisma, which are also
mirrored here.

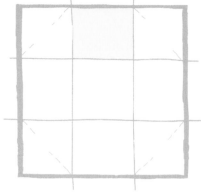

68 Basic Teachings

Houses breathe. Qi penetrates through windows and doors, and should be allowed to freely meander through a room. However, there are several factors that negatively influence Feng Shui, including clutter, straight lines or sharp edges, and corners.

Clutter

According to Feng Shui teachings, a messy house indicates a disjointed life. If a stack of old newspapers or a pile of dirty laundry hinders the flow of Qi over a long period of time, Sha Qi will impose its negative influence on other areas, making you tired and even depressed.

A congested entrance indicates a lack of openness toward new things. A mess under the bed may well keep you from getting a good night's sleep. Such "blockages" also occur when you postpone paying bills or making an unpleasant phone call. Check your pockets: If you find ticket stubs, sweet wrappers or old receipts, throw them away!

70

Long, Straight Passageways

Long, straight areas in your living space can have negative repercussions. They accelerate the flow of Qi so that it rushes through them instead of staying around. Long, straight corridors in an apartment can also speed up Qi. Combat this by clever positioning of accessories such as furniture, lamps or plants in a way that invites Qi to meander through more smoothly.

71

Qi will escape directly if there are two windows, or a door and window, situated opposite each other. Again, it can be diverted and kept in the room by adeptly arranged furniture, plants or lamps.

72

Sharp Edges

Sharp corners generate Sha Qi, which can have a negative influence on people. Especially avoid placing a bed near such corners. Always look for furniture with rounded corners, or where corners cannot be avoided, place plants in front of them.

73

Influences

There are several ways to positively influence Qi, thereby improving and harmonising the corresponding aspect of life. These only make sense, however, if you carefully analyse what you would like to change or influence in advance. Just as a wind chime does not influence Qi, but simply indicates that it is flowing, before placing mirrors in a room you should be clear about whether your aim is to strengthen Qi or to divert Sha Qi.

Mirrors

Mirrors are the simplest Feng Shui aid. Be aware of advantageous mirroring, such as reflected trees. If positioned correctly, they can make a room can appear larger and thereby positively influence Qi.

75

Make sure that your mirrors are
not tinted and are free of blind spots
or cracks. Mirrored tiles are not
recommended.

Ba-Gua Mirrors

Ba-Gua mirrors are round mirrors mounted in an octagonal frame. They are most often small and unassuming, with the eight trigrams painted on the frame. These mirrors are not usually implemented for their reflection, but because of the power of the trigrams to drive away evil. As such, they are often positioned directly opposite unfavourable locations to drive away Sha Qi.

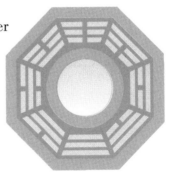

Octagonal Mirrors

Octagonal mirrors that are mounted to reflect images or are used as decorations can, of course, be larger as is appropriate to their function. They are usually positioned at the entrance to a home or a room.

78

Concave Mirrors

Concave mirrors collect and focus light. If you see yourself in one, you will only recognise your face. Because of this property, they are ideal for focusing Qi. Caution: As Sha Qi can also be bundled, find out exactly where the mirror will be most useful.

79

Convex Mirrors

Convex mirrors disperse light. If you look at yourself in one, you will see the whole room, not just your face. They are therefore ideally suited for diverting and dispersing Sha Qi.

80

Other polished objects, reflective spheres or a gong can be used in the same way as mirrors.

Crystals

If you would like to use a crystal to improve the flow of Qi, make sure that you concentrate the ray of light on an area you would like to strengthen.

82

Never move a crystal, as that may
cause it to "lose its concentration."

Crystals can be used in dark rooms by hanging them in a doorway still accessible to natural light. The glass prisms will refract the light and redirect it at the otherwise dark walls, thus activating the energy in the room.

It does not matter whether you use a diamond or a crystal made of glass or plastic, as long as it is a clear and well ground sphere. The effect you would like the crystal to have is also important.

84

Colours

Colours create atmosphere and specific effects: they provide energy or have a muting effect, whether they are used in interior design through wallpaper, carpets and home accessories, or in clothing.

Different colour combinations will vary the effects.
As a rule, the more intense a colour is, the less you need to create the desired effect.

86

Brown

Brown denotes reliability, practicality and closeness to the earth. It helps people who tend to be confused create a peaceful, dispassionate atmosphere. A word of caution: people who move slowly and are thoughtful should avoid brown, as it will practically immobilise them.

87

Green

Green is open to extraordinarily diverse interpretations, and several shades are worthy of mention. On the one hand, the colour symbolises equilibrium, harmony and peace. Combined with red, green is the colour of growth. It promotes healing, reduces worrying and disperses calm. The desire to travel and also—careful!—jealousy are stimulated by green.

An overabundance of green can lead to stagnation, however. The classic "hospital green" should definitely be avoided!

Emerald green has a slightly different interpretation:

It is a lively, stimulating colour, but not in any way anxiety-provoking.

Turquoise

Turquoise belongs to Yin and is very close to Wood-Qi. It creates a relaxed, yet lively and uplifting atmosphere.

90

Black

Black represents your career and symbolises money and power (together with pink it represents social power; together with yellow it stands for intellectual power).

People who wear a lot of black often would like to receive more attention. Keep your eyes open for this amongst family and friends!

Blue

Blue signalises spirituality, carefulness, consideration for others, caring, belief, steadfastness, loyalty, trustworthiness and solidarity. Blue "cools down" and calms, and helps create a harmonious atmosphere. Introverted people tend to wear blue.

Grey

Grey is the colour of self-denial, fear and depression.

Apart from this, it has a very formal character. Anxious people should take care to avoid wearing grey.

Orange

Orange represents social activity, supports joyful "togetherness" and generates constructive energy. It promotes a casual and relaxed atmosphere, even in dark areas. People who like to "go with the flow" are generally attracted to orange.

Pink

Pink is associated with romance and love. If you feel unwell or are down, pink has healing properties and provides warmth and comfort.

How about a bouquet of flowers in different shades of pink to lift your mood? Treat yourself to one sometime!

94

Purple

Purple is the colour of philosophers and dreamers, orators, poets and visionaries. Its connotations stem from that: high ideals, loyalty, truth and love are associated with it.

Purple is also considered a lucky colour.

95

Red

Red is not only the colour of life, it is also the colour that brings the most luck. The automatic associations are growth, joy, passion, love and virtues. It has been said that red is powerful enough to ward off evil forces.

Caution: Red has very strong energy and should therefore not be used by hyperactive or very emotional people.

97

White

The interpretations of white are divided. In China, white is the colour of mourning and is therefore not used frequently. In the Western world, white denotes purity, innocence, naivety and openness. If you want to be seduced, white is the colour to wear.

Excessive white in your living space should be avoided, however. Although it gives you room to think and develop without distractions, it can also prevent you from formulating clear opinions.

Yellow

Yellow symbolises the
attributes control, wisdom,
patience and tolerance.

It has a collective effect
and simultaneously stimu-
lates spiritual energy.

Violet

Violet is very close to the element Fire.
It brings passion into a room and
therefore promotes sociability. Depending
on the situation, just a few accessories in
this colour may be enough.

Light Blue

Light blue provides a restrained flow of energy that is normally agitated. It has a slightly calming effect, and should be used in bathrooms and kitchens. In addition, light blue makes rooms that receive little natural light appear bright and friendly.

100

Lavender

Lavender is too pale to provoke strong feelings, but it creates a mildly stimulating aura, and is therefore beneficial for social gatherings.

101

102

Hot Pink

Fashionable bright pink is not everyone's cup of tea and tends to be subject to the ebb and flow of current trends.

Pink intensifies a youthful, playful atmosphere. Clothes in this colour are best left to be worn by young people, or worn in small amounts as details.

Apricot

Pale apricot is closest to Earth energy, the central point, and as such is perfect for bedrooms, dispersing warmth and cosiness. A stronger shade, tending toward coral, can make living rooms warm and inviting.

103

104

Your choice of colour is important not only at home, but also when you make contact with other people. Plan the colour of your clothes to have the desired impact on the people you will meet.

Wear a combination of black and red when you are looking for an intensely passionate relationship and want to express it!

105

Are you looking for a new partner? Preferably someone you can have an intellectual relationship with? Wear black and yellow accents to catch that someone's attention.

Purple combined with black is a more spiritual combination. A purple scarf or bag are often enough to express your feelings.

106

107

Colours can not only be combined, they can also be elements of patterns. Basic patterns are closely connected to the five elements:

Irregular patterns	Water
Vertical stripes	Wood
Stars	Fire
Checks	Earth
Rounded forms	Metal

108

When color is combined with illustrations, their effects are intensified. Always be sure that the pictorial images (flowers, fruit, animals) or symbolic images (moon, sun, stars) conjure up positive associations for you! Choose wallpaper carefully, as it will be around for a while.

109

Ceilings of rooms should never be painted in dark shades. That would paralyse all energy, and the ceiling would literally press down on the inhabitants. Even Feng Shui and appropriate lighting can only alleviate such a situation to a certain extent.

If you are tired but nevertheless want to boost your creativity, surround yourself with bright colours. Details such as cushions, a picture, a tablecloth, candles or a bouquet of flowers are enough to provide colourful accents. Pale colours are less stimulating.

110

111

Light

Light greatly affects our well being. Too much, however, is not a good thing, whether the light is natural or artificial.

112

Ensure that a room does not have too many sources of natural light, because although Qi enters through them, they are also the route by which Qi escapes just as quickly. If a window provides sufficient light, it may make sense to keep the door closed or to darken another window to prevent the centre of the room from being dark, or the creation of dark corners. These are sure signs that Qi is flowing out too quickly. The effectiveness of light sources can be influenced by using mirrors.

113

Light can help you activate an aspect of life that,
according to the Ba-Gua scheme,
is not receiving sufficient attention.

Avoid using florescent lights; their flickering has a
negative influence. Candles collect energy
and give a much more pleasant light.

115

Always be careful how you direct
sources of light. As a rule, light travels
downward, so it can make sense to
light a room, a sculpture or
a piece of furniture from below
in order to avoid creating shadows.

Lampshades direct light both down- and upward. Ensure that the light does not shine directly at eye-level so no one is blinded.

116

117

The entrance to a house or apartment should never be too dark, as it can hinder in-flowing energy. If the hallway is too small or has no natural light source, use ceiling spotlights and a mirror to optically lighten and expand the space. This also offers guests a friendlier welcome!

Lamps should never be hung directly over your head, as they can have an oppressive and even disquieting effect. The use of florescent lighting tubes should be avoided, as the frequency of their flickering does not enhance our well being; it usually results in headaches.

118

Ideally, there should be sufficient daylight in the workplace, since no energy will flow without it. In the evenings it is advisable to light just your workplace and leave the rest of the room in subdued light. Deliberately directed sources of light help us focus our concentration on the task we are supposed to be doing, and help us to concentrate without becoming tense.

Light can help to activate Qi in a room.

Spotlights are brilliant for lighting up dark corners and allowing Qi to flow, thus avoiding a potential stagnation of the energy flow, while at the same time preventing depression and the lack of orientation often experienced in closed areas of a living space.

120

121

Metal, glass or other reflective lampshade materials create a very tense atmosphere. Select lampshades made of paper, as they provide a soft, indirect light that protects the eyes and encourages relaxation. The colour of the lampshade will influence your mood.

122

Sound

The sound of a windchime can help you relax, and signalises that Qi is flowing. Whether you choose wooden or metal chimes, the best place to hang them is outside, i.e., in front of a window, on a balcony or in a garden.

Water collects energy and the sound of splashing has a calming effect. A small fountain, either indoors or in the garden, can have a refreshing and cleansing effect. Choose its location carefully, as you should avoid having too much water in the area of Health.

124

Moving Objects

Mobiles or other moving objects indicate that energy is flowing and help disperse Qi in various directions. They are useful anywhere you would like to divert Qi.

125

Heavy Objects

such as stone statues can help combat feelings of insecurity. A heavy object can "ground" an uninhabited room and consolidate relationships. A heavy clock (metal) placed in the Career area can have a possitive effect.

126

Personal Element

People live in relation to their surroundings. Before using various aspects of Feng Shui to organise your environment, you should determine your own Feng Shui element, to see what role you play in the interaction of the elements. This is calculated using your birth date.

Your personal Feng Shui element can be determined by using your personal number, which is derived from the numbers representing the month and year of your date of birth. The year is calculated differently for women and men.

Since Chinese spring starts on the 4th of February, it is not in conjunction with the Gregorian calendar and you should beware of the following: If your birthday is on or before the 3rd of February you have to subtract one from the double digit year of your birth. Those born after February 4th maintain the unchanged double digit number.

128

129

Men obtain their year number by dividing the last two numbers of the birth year by 9. This will result in a quotient and remainder. If the remainder is 0 it is replaced with a 9; anything else stays as it is. Subtract the remainder from 10, and the difference is the year number.

Example:

A man was born on 31/1/1967.

—the last two digits of 1967 are	67
the date of birth is before 3. February, so subtract 1	66
—66 divided by 9	7, remainder 3
—10 - 3	7
—the year number is	7

130

Women calculate their year number by adding 5 to the last two digits of their birth year. The resulting sum is divided by 9, resulting in a quotient and remainder. The remainder is the year number.
If the remainder is 0, the woman's year number is 9.

女

Example:

A woman was born on 19/8/1962.

—the last 2 digits of 1962 are	62
—add 5	67
—67 divided by 9 is	7, remainder 4
—the year number is	4

The month number is calculated with the help of this table:

If your birthday is on or after:	Your month number is
5. January	12
5. February	1
5. March	2
4. April	3
5. May	4
5. June	5
7. July	6
6. August	7
7. September	8
9. October	9
7. November	10
6. December (through 4. January)	11

The intersection of your month and year numbers is your personal Feng Shui number.

Month number	Year number	1 2 3 4 5 6 7 8 9
1		8 2 5 8 2 5 8 2 5
2		7 1 4 7 1 4 7 1 4
3		6 9 3 6 9 3 6 9 3
4		5 8 2 5 8 2 5 8 2
5		4 7 1 4 7 1 4 7 1
6		3 6 9 3 6 9 3 6 9
7		2 5 8 2 5 8 2 5 8
8		1 4 7 1 4 7 1 4 7
9		9 3 6 9 3 6 9 3 6
10		8 2 5 8 2 5 8 2 5
11		7 1 4 7 1 4 7 1 4
12		6 9 3 6 9 3 6 9 3

Example: the year number of a man who was born on 31/1/1967 is 7, his month number is 12, so his personal Feng Shui number is 6.

The year number of a woman born on 19/8/1962 is 4, her month number is 7, so her personal Feng Shui number is 2.

133

Here you can ascertain your personal Feng Shui element and direction.

Personal number	Element	Direction
1	Water	North
2	Earth	Southwest
3	Wood	East
4	Wood	Southeast
5 (Men)	Earth	Northeast
5 (Women)	Earth	Southwest
6	Metal	Northwest
7	Metal	West
8	Earth	Northeast
9	Fire	South

Your element can tell you a great
deal about your personality, including
how you relate to certain places,
buildings and to other people.

135

Re-examine your home, this time taking into account your personal element. Even if you are planning a move, you can gather lots of information about your future home in advance. You influence your surroundings, just as they influence you. Not all surroundings have a positive effect on everyone.

A Wood location is usually marked by pillars and heights, faces toward the east, and is dominated by the colour green. The surroundings are characterised by dense forest with tall trees in rural areas, and by tall buildings in urban areas.

136

137

A Wood person and Wood location complement each other nicely. This is a place where creativity flourishes, one that is also ideal for teaching. It will bring you good luck.

138

A Fire person is nourished by a Wood location—a stimulating combination. Career and employment can be positively influenced, but you are more likely to gain fame than money.

139

Earth people are weakened by Wood locations, as Wood will deplete their energy. Fire elements, such as the colour red, can help to liven up this constellation.

140

The positive connection between Metal and Wood is short-lived. It is soon time to change something again; a Fire person should count on moving soon.

141

A Wood location is ideal for a Water person, especially for those engaged in professions involving communication or mediation.

Fire locations face south and are characterised by the colour red. Buildings tend to have sharp corners and edges, and the surroundings are dominated by triangular shapes, such as views of mountains or houses with pointed roofs.

142

143

Wood and Fire have a short-term positive influence on each other. For a time the location will inspire Wood people, but financial gain should not be anticipated. Prepare, rather, for a move in the near future.

144

A Fire location is ideal for Fire people. It fuels their ambition and career.

An Earth person will feel comfortable in a Fire location. Wealth, Family and Children will be positively influenced.

145

146

As Metal is melted by Fire, be wary of combining these two elements! You can count on a decrease in fortune where a Metal person coincides with a Fire location. If this applies to you, try to "ground" the combination by using clay- or terracotta-coloured accessories or flowerpots.

147

Fire and Water conflict with each other. Water people living in a Fire location should be prepared for arguments and trouble. Lessen the effects by introducing Metal elements. Paint your walls white!

The characteristics of an Earth location are flat roofs, the colours yellow and ochre, and locations facing northeast or southwest. The surrounding landscape is flat. In urban areas this could be a district of primarily bungalow construction.

148

149

Wood people feel most at home in Earth locations. Just as trees draw nourishment from the earth, over time Wood people will deplete an Earth location of its vitality and creativity. Fire elements, especially red, can invigorate the atmosphere.

150

The interaction between Earth and Fire can be very harmonious. Ambitious people should expect a change of location, however, as they will be unable to fully develop their creativity in an Earth location.

151

Earth and Earth are ideal partners, or so it would seem. This initially stable situation can develop more toward stubbornness and dogmatism.

152

A Metal person can benefit greatly from an Earth location; both elements positively affect each other. This situation offers many opportunities waiting to be made use of. You can expect success in both business and private matters.

153

The combination of Earth and Water produces mud and polluted water. An Earth location is therefore disadvantageous to Water people in every way.

154

Metal locations are characterised by rounded architectural elements, such as window arches or bay windows, and the buildings usually face west or northwest. The dominant colours are white, silver, gold or grey. The surroundings are hilly and characterised by domes.

155

The properties of Metal locations are unfavourable for Wood people.
Accidents are to be feared, but the element Water can help prevent them.
Small fountains in rooms or dark-blue cushions can have a
positive influence on the combination.

156

As Fire melts
Metal, Metal people
should avoid Fire
locations.

157

Earth people feel very much at home
in Metal locations, as the elements
positively influence each other. Although
you will not become affluent, you can
expect to enjoy both your work and
a harmonious family life.

158

Metal locations are favourable for Metal people. Success in the areas
of Career, Children, Fame, Knowledge and Ancestors/Family
are to be expected.

159

Metal locations will help Water people achieve success in their careers, especially in professions dealing with financial transactions, communication and media. Family ties are also stable.

160

Buildings facing north that have a large proportion of glass and in which the colours blue and black dominate are Water locations. The surroundings are marked by ponds, lakes or rivers, though buildings with lots of glass can take over this role in an urban environment.

161

Water locations have a stimulating effect on the creativity and artistic ability of Wood people, but also on their family planning.

162

Where Water meets Fire, flames are extinguished. The same applies to Fire people in Water locations. Money, luck, harmony, fun and satisfaction will stay away. Move to a different location as fast as possible, but until then, counteract the negative effects by removing dark colours and replacing them with pale shades of green.

163

Water and Earth tend to turn to mud. Sight is occluded and agreements must be written down in order to avoid misunderstandings. Round-shaped objects of the element Metal can help here.

164

A Water location is good for a Metal person, particularly in relation to your workplace. But beware: You will tend to waste money!

165

Although a Water person feels comfortable in a Water location, her or his absence will be be most noticeable, because their flowing character is promoted here. The prerequisites for success look favourable.

166 Introduction to the Practice

There is no such thing as the ideal workplace or home. As a rule, we live in certain conditions over which we have little influence. Feng Shui shows us how to use simple means to come just a little closer to the ideal situation, such as choosing the right material, correct positioning, or by using plants, colours, mirrors or light to optimise the Qi in our surroundings. What should you avoid? What should be observed in designing the interior of individual rooms and areas of life? Feng Shui provides valuable guidelines.

Feng Shui rule number one: clean and tidy! Rooms crammed full of junk tend to block and impede the fruitful interaction between individual energy fields. Energy must be able to flow. Before analysing your situation, clear away the mess: You will be surprised to see how many problems disappear and how few aids are still necessary to set positive energy free.

Checklist for Cleaning Up:

- Commit yourself to clearing away the mess
- Decide on a starting date and write it in your calendar
- Set yourself a realistic goal—decide in advance how much you want to do and achieve
- Make a timetable
- Have bags and boxes at hand to dispose of the rubbish
- Work behind closed doors
- Before starting, take a few minutes to sit down and relax
- Work from the top to the bottom
- Have you got too much of everything? Part with it, even if it hurts! Decide as you go along—what purpose does a thing serve? Is it instrumental to your well being?
- A good exercise is to get rid of one object a day.
- Only acquire new things after ridding yourself of the old ones.

168

In which areas of life can Feng Shui be useful?

The aim of Feng Shui is restore balance and harmony in all areas of life, whether in regard to your career, your health, or how you treat your family, friends and colleagues, as well as in designing your home and garden. Feng Shui can help to create the conditions for harmony and success in all these areas.

169

Am I the only one who is affected, or will others notice the change in my environment?

Implement the changes inspired by Feng Shui carefully. Changes you undertake are tailored to have an optimal effect on you, personally, but everyone in your home or workplace will notice the positive influences in an indirect form.

Can mistakes occur in the Feng Shui instructions that could result in negative influences?

You can protect yourself by trying out changes and observing your reactions before undertaking a "radical cure."

Before re-wallpapering your bedroom and changing the curtains, for example, test the new colour by placing pillows of that colour in the room. Do you still like the colour a few days later? Does it lift your mood? Carefully contemplate the consequences of your changes.

171

Should I immediately put into practice all the tips that are relevant to the area of my life I want to improve?

Set priorities so that you can develop a feel for the measures, and to allow interactions among them grow into a harmonious "whole." Start with the room you use most, or turn to the aspect of life you currently find most important. If it is your career, you should apply your energy to that part of your home.

Start with individual steps and you will quickly experience positive results. Continue until you have completed your task. The result will be a harmonious whole that will fully unfold its influence over time.

How do you know if Feng Shui is working? When do you see initial results?

It is possible that you do not notice the effects straightaway, because the process takes a little longer and you will have to get used to the changes first. The first signs could be that you feel a sense of release, can sleep better, or that your friends are particularly impressed with your party, for instance.

172

173

The Entrance to Your Home

If you have a front yard or other entrance from the street to your house, make sure the path leading to the front door is not straight, but slightly curved. It should be broader near the street and narrower as you approach the door. U-shaped paths or paths with flower beds in the middle are also favourable. They prevent uncontrolled energy from hitting the entrance area. Qi is quickly lost on wide driveways or paths. Lamps at the entrance help to channel the flow of energy.

174

Does your front garden have a fence or hedge with a gate? A metal gate with upward-pointing elements on the outside will bring you luck. Concrete spheres or decorative figurines on the gate posts will protect your property. It does not matter whether these are the classic Chinese "guardian" figures, such as dragons, or modern terracotta figures of your choice. It is only important that they face forward.

175

In your entryway, as well, cleanliness is of the utmost importance. Objects left lying about create a blockade and prevent fortuitous opportunities from reaching you. Apart from this, they are not exactly an inviting sight for visitors.

Water in front of a house attracts favourable opportunities. Where possible, have a small pond or fountain in your front yard. Always keep the water clean so you do not attract negative Sha. If the pond is quite close to the house, a small, winding path leading to it will make the distance seem greater. The path should be made of a material that is appealing but unassuming. An area of light gravel, for instance, is easy to care for and creates positive associations with the sea, a bearer of good luck.

177

A roof over the entryway protects it from wind and precipitation and gives it a more finished appearance. However, its sharp angles also divert positive Qi away from the house and shoot "poisonous arrows" at your home. If a more favourable design is not possible, it is better not to construct one at all.

Drainpipes or conspicuous piping are often covered with bars so that they do not become dirty and thus attract negative energy. The pipes can be hidden with potted plants filled with pretty flowers to counteract any rising Sha.

178

179

If you live in a multi-family house, make sure the stairway is well lit. This not only provides a friendly welcome for guests and people coming home, it also helps positive energy spread out in the entryway. The same applies to the area outside your home: A soft light in front of the house promotes positive Qi. It should not be too close to the front door, however, so as not to interfere with the flow of energy.

The Front Door

The main stream of energy travels into and out of a home through the front door, which represents the most important connection between home and the outside world. The door should be straight and not squeak or stick at all—it should always be easy to open and close so that the harmony of the inhabitants is not endangered.

The appearance of the front door is immensely important.

The varnish must be fresh and shiny. This not only gives visitors a favourable impression, but also contributes to a constant flow of money.

A front door should never be made completely of glass. Half is enough, otherwise too much energy will flow in and out. A lattice or light curtains pane can help combat this. In addition, hang a crystal in the window.

182

Front doors should never directly face the corners of the building opposite, as they point to the door like razor-blades, creating negative Sha. Your front door should also not face a gap between two buildings, as capital can flow away from you through this opening if it is not obstructed by an artificial barrier, such as a hedge.

183

Take care to keep all metal objects on your door polished, such as letterboxes, house numbers, metal fittings, doorknobs or knockers. Only reflecting metal wards off negative energy.

As far as you are able to choose a house door, select one which is large enough—at least as large as the doors to the rooms in the house, in order to maintain proportions. This maximizes the flow of Qi to the interior of your home. Avoid placing windows or balcony doors opposite the front door, so that energy does not simply "charge" through the house creating drafts that may negatively affect your health.

Ideally, your door should open so that people walk into an enclosed entryway, rather than coming up against a wall.

Windows positioned next to the front door can have unfavourable consequences; here, too, you can use curtains or plants with rounded leaves to prevent the intrusion of unexpected events. Are there windows near the entrance that might be inviting to burglars? Cacti placed here will ward off unwelcome visitors. The negative effect of the prickly plants that is best avoided in the area of Relationships is perfectly appropriate here!

186

Electric doorbells disperse electro-smog and create imbalanced Qi. Bells with soft ringing tones help clear the atmosphere and are more pleasant to the ear.

Test

- How do you feel when you approach your entrance?
- What do you pass and how are the objects aligned (high, low, near)?
- Is it easy to find the entrance? Are there clearly defined paths?
- Actively perceive the sounds, smells and sights
- Imagine that this is your first visit. How do you feel?
- What awaits you when you enter your home?

If you carry out this exercise carefully and seriously it can tell you a great deal about the quality of the Qi surrounding your home.

187

188 Which direction does your front door face, and what import does that have?

- East: Growth, health, initiative find their way in.
- Southeast: A clear emphasis on finances!
- South: Financial success, happiness and friendship.
- Southwest: Relationships; mount a wind chime to ward off sickness, just in case.
- West: A quiet but constant flow of energy is certain; favourable opportunities can enter easily.
- Northwest: The inhabitants' characteristics will be diligence, energy and the desire to travel.
Caution: Keep an eye on your money!
- North: Prosperity, but cold energy that has an immobilising effect can also enter.
- Northeast: Knowledge, education and the ghosts of ancestors can enter; hanging Ba-Gua mirrors can protect you.

189

"We shape our buildings,

thereafter they shape us."
(Winston Churchill)

190 Foyer/Entryway

Foyers should ideally be bright, or at least well lit, not too narrow, and always clear and tidy. Qi needs space to spread out and unfold its positive effects. If the entrance is too narrow or dark, a mirror can give the illusion of more space. A plant will provide energy. One's first glimpse should be aesthetically pleasing. Since the entrance is your home's "calling card," decorate it tastefully and sparsely.

191

A long, narrow, and in the worst case also dark entryway will provide for the least favourable flow of energy. Place plants alternately along both walls of the hallway to brake the Qi and promote circulation. Mirrors and dimmed lights will contribute to the desired effect.

Stairs inside your home should never lead directly to the front door—this makes it too easy for energy to escape! Spiral staircases are poison, as they bore a hole into the core of your house and their curve accelerates the stream of energy moving away from living areas.

192

Living Room

The living room is usually the central room of the home, where the majority of activities take place and where guests are received. Every visitor gleans their own personal impression of you and your family from this room, so it should radiate light and friendliness.

The living room is often the locus of much of family life, and a place you can relax after a day's work by reading, watching television or listening to music. Warmth and cosiness are the basis for relaxation in this room.

Since many people use this room at the same time, be prepared to go to great lengths to attain a harmonious atmosphere in it.

194

As a rule, the living room is the largest room in a home. The most important aspect of ideal living is space: The centre of the room should always remain uncluttered. Qi has to move around the furniture in order to circulate and develop optimally.

Qi tends to stagnate in overcrowded rooms—you yourself will feel uncomfortable and inhibited, as if there is not enough air to breathe. A general formula would be: Use fewer items of furniture and avoid large, heavy pieces. Voluptuous curtains, thick cushions or an excess of decorative objects have no place here.

Sensibly designed seating corners promote sociability and a harmonious family life.

Choose several seating options rather than a single sofa, so that everyone can chose the spot where they feel most comfortable.

Sofas and chairs should face the centre of the room. Regardless of whether you have chosen a square or circular formation, the backs of sofas should always face a wall. Seating should never be placed with its back toward a window or door—this fosters insecurity, as you have no control over who enters or leaves the room. Be sure to choose a seat from which you have a complete overview of the room.

Never place furniture diagonally in a corner. The walls would literally bear down on anyone seated there.

196

Seating should be rounded to avoid Qi that cuts.

Soft material ensures relaxation. Avoid sharp edges or corners or spiky plant leaves directed toward the person seated. "Diffuse" the situation by positioning plants with rounded leaves, cushions or tablecloths where you can.

Television

Electric devices emit negative Qi, even when switched off. To combat the harmful rays make sure that the television is never positioned near the seating arrangement—it should be completely separate.

To absorb negative energy, you can place an aquarium or plant next to the television. The harmful effects of the electromagnetic waves are best counteracted by keeping the television in a cabinet with doors that close.

The most appropriate floor covering is parquet, as the Wood energy ensures an even energy flow. When choosing carpets, try to restrict yourself to laying runners or area rugs so that they do not interrupt the flow of energy.

Wall-to-wall carpeting or large rugs are not advisable.

Wallpaper

Select light, inviting shades of cream or yellow for your living room. Pink, peach, shades of red, and orange create a warm and inviting atmosphere. Vertical stripes can make a room look higher and larger, while patterned wallpaper is ideal for rooms intended soley for relaxation and rejuvenation.

Plants

Plants with pointy leaves, such as the Yucca, should be placed in uninhabited corners, never next to sofas or armchairs in which guests are seated.

In addition to the possibility of harming someone, the pointy leaves cut positive Qi. Sharp table corners or shelves can be concealed with small plants that have rounded leaves.

201

Living room tables should be made of wood. Round or oval shapes inspire communication, while corners will separate people. Although glass tables make the room seem larger, the harsh noise of someone setting a glass on the table is less pleasant. If the table legs can be seen through the table top your guests are likely to think of getting up, which does not give a very welcoming impression.

Living rooms should be lit by means of indirect light. Standing lamps or ceiling flood lights will create upward striving energy. Single candles or candelabras create a cozy, peaceful atmosphere, focus peoples' attention, and inspire conversations.

As a rule, the living room should always be well lit.

202

The Position of Your Living Room Furthers Certain Activities:

A living room facing southeast is bright and lively, and will accordingly stimulate all activity.

Living rooms facing south are well suited for parties and large social gatherings, but you will not find relaxation here.

Southwest-facing rooms offer a stable, comfortable atmosphere.

Rooms oriented toward the west provide for stimulating conversation and enjoyment, but also romance.

Unfortunately, you cannot always determine where your living room lies. Use whatever tools are available to design the feel of the room!

An indoor fountain or aquarium gives the living room a lively, fresh atmosphere, strengthening the energy flow. Choose goldfish or other red fish, as red is a symbol of good luck and prosperity.

205

Windows and Curtains

Windows should always be immaculately clean and clear; broken panes should be replaced immediately.

Sunlight streaming in stimulates the flow of energy, another reason to keep your curtains or blinds open in the daytime. When the sunlight is very intense, draw a light curtain to reduce the glare.

Never obstruct a window by hanging or placing too many things in front of it—along with doors, windows are the main entrance for positive Qi. Open all the windows in your home at least once a day!

It is not always possible or desirable to give your neighbours a full view into your home. Blinds are a good solution for small windows as they light in while blocking the view from outside. Wood has a neutral effect on Qi, Metal accelerates its flow, and synthetic materials block it.

Curtains overfill small rooms, but can make larger rooms very cozy. They are an ideal solution for bedrooms.

Window shutters block light and Qi completely.

Vertical screens have an effect similar to blinds, but make the room appear larger.

As in any room, doors and windows
should never face each other, as
energy will simply flow out and be lost.
Low book cases, plants or screens can
slow the energy down or hold it in the room
at least temporarily.

207

The Kitchen

Think carefully about the design of your kitchen. It should be functional but also easy to care for. A stove (Fire) and sink (Water) are the basic elements. At the same time, try to achieve a balance of all five elements, which have more contact with each other in this room than in any other.

208

209

Never put the sink next to the stove—Fire and Water negatively influence each other and will bring bad luck. Placing a cabinet containing pots and pans (Metal) between them, for instance, will dampen the effect. Refrigerators and washing machines should also not be next to the stove.

210

Use the space above the stove to store earthenware (Earth) or steel pots (Metal), but never herbs or oils (Wood).

211

Never lay carpet, PVC or linoleum in the kitchen. A stone floor or tiles bring the element Earth into the room, harmoniously balancing the strong presence of Wood (food), Water, Fire and Metal (kitchen equipment).

Never use a rubbish bin without a
lid, and make sure to empty it as often as
possible—preferably daily!

212

213

Knives should never be hung or lie about exposed in the room because of the Sha Qi that emanates from them. They should be stored in a knife block or a drawer.

214

The atmosphere in a kitchen should be light and welcoming. Closed cabinets are better than open shelves.

Ideally, the cabinets and work surfaces in your kitchen should have rounded corners.

215

216

Exhaust fans above the stove should be avoided, as they suck the Qi out of the room. As an alternative, open windows to allow fresh air to enter and thus stimulate the flow of Qi.

Dining Room

The dining table is the focal point of a dining room. It should be round, oval or octagonal depending on what the space in your home allows, but never made of glass.

218

Wood is the perfect element for the dining room and can be brought into the room in the form of furniture. As the food served deserves our full attention, avoid overloading any cabinets or display cases to the point that they become a distraction.

Refrain from using aggressive symbols, and avoid edges or corners. Pictures with festive motifs or of happy people always contribute to a harmonious atmosphere.

219

220

You should not be able to see the front door, the kitchen or the bathroom from your dining room. Where this is architecturally not possible, block the view by hanging curtains, blinds or strings of beads.

Extravagant table decor can inhibit dining room conversation. Make sure your centerpiece is not so high that it blocks people's view of each other.

221

Adeptly positioned mirrors
(hung opposite each other) allow energy
to bounce back and forth, livening up
dinner conversation.

222

223 Food

Nutrition

... Observe what is eaten and that with which one tries
to fill one's own mouth.

When bestowing care and nourishment, it is important that the
right people are provided for and that one provides for one's own
nourishment in the right way. In order to know someone, one need
only observe on whom she bestows her care and which aspects of her
own being she tends and nourishes. Nature nourishes all creatures.
A great person nourishes and cares for those who are industrious,
who will in turn take care of all people.

(I Ching/27)

In these hectic times it is important to have a room, or at least a place, where the family gathers once a day around a table to peacefully partake of a meal. Food should be enjoyed. When you take time to eat and relax, less harmful stomach acid is released.

224

225

Our surroundings play an important part at mealtimes. Which furnishings bring forth which moods?

The Business Meal:

A square table is formal and more likely to stimulate dynamic conversation than a rectangular table. A marble tabletop enhances this effect.

A Romantic Dinner for Two:

A round table promotes more activity than an oval table. A glass table top should be avoided in the home, but together with the correct decor it can be quite stimulating for this area.

The Family Table:

An oval-shaped table disperses a modified, soft type of Qi.

Light wood, such as pine, aids relaxation and promotes conversation.

228

Feng Shui-appropriate nutrition favours foods containing natural Qi, in other words, freshly prepared whole ingredients. Avoid parboiled, frozen or dried products.

The microwave is taboo (due to harmful electromagnetic waves), as are agricultural products cultivated using fertilisers. Meat should come only from animals kept in ecologically sound ways. Industrially refined sugar should be replaced with natural sweeteners, such as honey, that have a gentler impact on our blood sugar level.

Balanced nutrition will ensure a balance of Yin and Yang in the body. All five elements should be present in equal amounts in our diet.

The list shows the categorisation of nutrients, from the Yang category (top) to the Yin category (bottom):

YANG
Seasalt
Meat
Eggs
Chicken
Fish
Bread
Rice
Noodles
Beans
Milk products
Vegetables
Fruit
Sugar
Liquids
YIN

If you tend to be quick-tempered or easily feel frustrated (Yang emotions), Yin foods have a balancing effect on your temperament. If you tend toward depression, day-dreaming and sensitivity, Yang foods can help.

Each of the five elements corresponds to a particular taste and specific foods that should be part of a balanced diet:

Wood: sour. Examples: olives, vinegar, sauerkraut

Fire: bitter. Examples: spring onions, limes, chillies

Earth: sweet. Examples: fruit (pears, etc.), sweetcorn

Metal: spicy-hot. Examples: garlic, mustard, ginger

Water: salty. Examples: winter vegetables, sauces

Oils and Fats

Plant oil and fats, such as olive-oil, are preferable to animal fats. They cause less cholesterol to be deposited in the blood vessels, making clogged arteries and cardiac disease less likely.

Fish and Meat

The entire spectrum of fish and seafoods are an important part of nutrition according to Feng Shui and, due to their low calorie and fat content, are preferable to meat. Fish has a high protein content and is very easy to digest.

Fruit and Vegetables

In order to give your body the nutrients and Qi energy it needs, nothing is more important than eating a large variety of fruit and vegetables prepared in many different ways. Beans, nuts, legumes or tofu are particularly rich in protein.

Grains

The grains in bread, pasta or breakfast cereals should make up a large part of our diet. They contain carbohydrates, protein and fats, as well as essential vitamins and minerals. Whole grains such as rice or coarsely ground grains in bread are more nourishing than processed grains, as the greatest concentration of nutrients lies directly under the hull.

Eggs and Milk Products

Coconut and soy milk are preferable to cow milk for cooking, as milk products and eggs are rich in the saturated fats which can contribute to a higher cholesterol level.

235

236

Home Office

If at all possible, avoid having your
office in the bedroom.

237

Place your desk so that when you are seated at it your back is toward the wall and you have both the door and window(s) in view. You should not sit with your back toward windows or doors.

An L-shaped work area creates room for a computer and a surface for other tasks, or even storage.

陰

A neat desk increases your concentration. A crystal or fresh flowers on the edge of the desk have an invigorating effect.

239

240

Office away from Home

The location of your workplace already indicates a lot about the future of the business, and therefore also your opportunities for personal development. If the entrance of the building is located in a narrow road between two larger buildings opposite, there is a threat of the capital flowing away. This also applies to buildings situated at intersections or at a fork in the road.

If the corner of the building opposite points in the direction of the entrance to your workplace, it is a case of Sha: Profits will literally be cut, and the working atmosphere is not likely to be good.

241

242

If your workplace lies between two other, larger buildings, or if there is a hill opposite, there is a danger that Qi cannot enter. Favourable business deals will not materialise and profits will not flow into the enterprise.

An office building should never lie on the outside of a curve. If this is the case, the constant flow of positive Qi will be cut off.

A location on the inner side of the curve, however, promises success.

243

244

Well lit and easily accessible hallways in an office building ensure the free flow of positive energy to each office. Offices at the end of long, dark corridors are not to be recommended. The entrance to the offices of the management should be particularly wide and bright.

All the activities in an office building should take place on appropriate levels of the building: Directors should be located on higher floors than the middle-management or the other employees, in order to come into contact with the flow of favourable energy.

245

The same aids that help improve an unfavourable situation at home can be applied in your office. Plants not only serve to block unwelcome views, they also spread positive Qi, especially into dark corners that need more energy. Mirrors can allow you to immediately identify anyone entering, or make the room appear larger. Pleasant light, for example from a standing lamp, is also invigorating.

246

247

Is your desk opposite someone else's? Make your chair higher, so that you are figuratively on a higher level. In this way you will "look down" at your neighbour—an old trick to increase your self-confidence!

The same applies when visitors or clients take a seat in front of your desk.

248

The colour and shape of your desk can have wide-ranging effects:

A large, solid, dark desk is excellent for financial business, a square desk made of light wood serves new business, while a white or light grey desk with a soft shape promotes creativity.

Your desktop should never be too small.

249

The view from your workplace window may be inspiring, but will encourage your thoughts to wander. It can also blind you; it may be better to have the sun at your back. Natural light, the best option for offices, is not always available. In addition to artificial sources of light, slightly shiny office furniture or friendly pictures in reflective frames may help bring the sun into your office.

250

Proximity to electric equipment is not exactly beneficial for your health. If you work extensively with computers, you may not be able to escape this, but you can remove all extraneous electrical devices (such as clocks) from your workspace.

Plants near your computer work wonders. Also, the computer should not stand directly on your desk, but on a computer table next to it.

Even with the computer, you need to throw away your garbage! Only save what you really need. Set yourself the goal of ruthlessly deleting all redundant data every three months. This will make your computer work faster and allow your thoughts free reign.

251

252

Clean up! Nothing is more inspiring than a clear desk! Create a logical filing system. Piles of files block your capacity for thought— they belong in cabinets. Organising objects according to their energy content means the left side of the desk is for new projects, ideas, marketing and sales issues. The right side is reserved for bills, reports and lists. The area directly in front of you should remain completely clear.

253

A lot of effort is required to create a Feng Shui environment in an office-block workspace. Try to have a protected location—never have your back toward an open corridor or a doorway. If all else fails, a large jacket hung over the back of your chair will help.

The desk in front of you must remain clear.

A Tip for the "Worst Case":

Gather your personal Feng Shui set—your favourite office mug, a plant, fresh flowers, or photos of loved ones—and have it near your working space to improve the Qi and allow your creativity to take flight.

254

Always keep your office door shut.

An open door invites distraction, as do shelves at your back to which all of your colleagues have access. If there is more than one door to your office, two streams of Qi may collide with each other. Unfortunately, the effects can only be partially negated, but not eradicated, by putting up medium-high shelves or plants around the room.

256

Office furniture should be selected using the same criteria as for home furniture. Rounded corners are preferable, as they do not disperse Sha.

Where this is not possible, sharp corners can be concealed by plants. Overly full rooms or shelves can inhibit your thought processes and the circulation of Qi.

Cabinets and shelves should not be too high.

The circle of light from a bright desk lamp will help you concentrate on and channel your energy toward your work. The light should be even, without flickering, and not too bright.

257

Be careful that your office door does not open so that people entering face directly face your desk. The direct onslaught of Qi could make you out of sorts, and you can be seen by everyone. Nonetheless, you should be able to see who is entering your office. You should have everything under control.

If the room permits, position your desk in a corner so that you sit with your back to the wall.

259

Bedroom

Humans spend a large proportion of their lives in bed, so the arrangement of your bedroom deserves special attention. The bed should be your highest priority. Take care to position it so that it is not in direct view from a window or the door. Especially important is that the foot end does not face the door. If that is unavoidable, you may want to place a screen in front of it.

260

Mirrors in the bedroom are generally unfavourable. Most people have mirrors anyway to see themselves when getting dressed, but they should always be covered with a blanket or curtain before you go to sleep.

Cabinets or shelves over the head of your bed, or slanted ceilings or beams above the bed weigh down on your body, causing you to wake up exhausted. Avoid such constellations whenever possible.

261

262

If you have direct access from the bedroom to the bathroom, the door should at least be behind a corner. Take care not to have the foot end of your bed facing the door, or if space does not allow that, place a cupboard, Spanish wall, or Japanese screen between the bed and the door.

263

You can only sleep as well as your bed allows! Make sure your mattress and bed frame are made of natural materials. Futons and beds with wooden frames are ideal. The frame should be about 60 cm/24 inches high.

264

Waterbeds can disturb your sleep, as they are a destructive combination of Water and Metal.

The metal content in an iron bedframe can inhibit your sleep because it charges itself electro-magnetically.

Canopies over the bed isolate you and make it more difficult to get up.

The bedroom ceiling should always be painted a lighter shade than the walls.

A dark ceiling will seem lower and restrict the flow of energy.

265

Rounded shapes and corners inhibit the
accrual of negative Qi. A plant in the
bedroom will refresh the energy.

267

The television does not belong in the bedroom!
If this cannot be avoided, at least be sure it is placed
in a cabinet or covered when not in use.

A solid headboard, a firm expanse of mattress and comfortable access to the bed from both sides can positively affect a relationship.

268

269

Never have pictures of your children in your bedroom—keep this realm child-free! Instead, hang up pictures of happy occasions, such as weddings or other celebrations.

270

Sleeping Arrangements

Which direction does your head point when you sleep? Check the location of your bed and correct it, if necessary:

South is positive for people whose work is intellectually or creatively stimulating, who have to study, or who need to concentrate on writing.

If your head points southeast, your body will take up streams of energy that can positively affect your finances or relationships of any sort.

Southwest should be avoided at all costs—it will harm your health and cannot be positively counteracted by any Feng Shui aids.

272

273

Good news for all those who suffer from sleeping disorders: Point your bed to the north and finally get a good nights' sleep! If your bedroom does not permit this, find some opportunity to sleep heading north for four weeks at a time to "recover." You will sleep more deeply and peacefully for some period of time afterward.

Northeast promises restless nights, but
will fire your ambition.

274

Sleeping toward the northwest helps to improve your organisational abilities and makes you think more clearly. This direction is particularly beneficial to those who are worried about providing for their families.

276

Restless sleepers feel exhausted the following morning and feel the urge to stay in bed all day. If this seems familiar, try to sleep with your head toward the east. You will wake up refreshed and well rested, a bonus for all those who wish to advance their career.

277

People who feel stressed, nervous and irritated should sleep with their heads pointing west. They will relax and find satisfaction.

Children's Rooms

A child's rooms mirrors the whole house, whether one or more children occupy the room. This is where they play with their siblings or friends, do their homework and sleep. All these needs have to be taken into account when choosing colours, materials and furniture.

279

Sleep

The door to your children's bedroom should remain closed at night. Make sure that the curtains are closed or the blinds down, in order to restrict the flow of energy and allow your child to sleep deeply. The head of the bed should never be under a window, as the incoming energy is too strong and could inhibit their sleep. Ideally, the head end and one side of the bed will be next to a wall. This position imparts peace and security.

If several children sleep in the same room, the beds should all face the same direction—the Sandman will appear a lot sooner!

280

When choosing children's beds, make sure that they are made of wood, so that harmful Qi cannot get its foot in the door. The bed linens should also be made of natural materials; there is a wide array of child-friendly patterns. Avoid lively pictures on pillow-cases!

Provide plenty of cozy cushions and soft blankets—children's beds should be particularly inviting to sleep in.

281

What is true for the rest of the house also applies to the children's bedroom—it should never be crammed full of things. Children will feel oppressed and unconcentrated in the midst of clutter. Clear rooms offer more space to play and dance around!

Storage in underbed boxes, colourful boxes or wagons help to keep order. They are also the right height for children to reach, and make straightening up much easier.

Children's furniture should never be large and dark—the room should remain light and roomy. Tables and chairs with rounded corners reduce the danger of injuries, and are less likely to cut positive energy or generate negative energy.

Wood is an ideally suited material.

282

Televisions, computers and other electrical devices do not belong in children's rooms!

Children are particularly sensitive to the electro-magnetic waves they emit.

284

Which of your child's characteristics would you like to enhance, and which would you rather curb?

Bright colours have a stimulating effect and will instigate mental activity, especially the Yang colours of red, yellow and orange. Soft, pastel, Yin colours are calming and will create a happy but relaxed atmosphere.

285

Toys made of wood are not only durable, but also offer pleasurable sensory experiences. Infants, especially, enjoy the feel of wood. All toys should be cleared away from the children's bedroom at night so they cannot interfere with the energy flow.

Mobiles should never hang directly over your child's head, but they can be hung near the foot of the bed. The mobile will be easier to see and less easily torn down. Shimmering, metal objects have an animating effect, whereas soft materials in pale colours are more soothing.

286

287

Children's thirst for knowledge is increased by
hanging a crystal in the northeast part of the room,
which is the Knowledge sector. Encourage your child to
read by placing a reading lamp on the bedside table.
Of course, it shouldn't be switched off too late.....

Bathroom

In the context of Feng Shui practice, the bathroom is traditionally negative: It serves the removal of refuse and getting clean. The bathroom is also used for relaxation, however. The whole setup is symbolic of our health. At the same time, the energy flowing in this room can be said to represent our financial situation.

In any case, the bathroom remains the most intimate area of the home and should be treated as such.

289

When choosing a new home, try to select one in which there is not a toilet next to the kitchen, the dining room, or opposite the main entrance. This is not only because of unpleasant smells that arise— energy would flow away directly through the various pipes.

For hygienic reasons, toilets should not be situated in the interior part of the home. Light and fresh air are a must, and in addition to their pleasant qualities, help combat dampness and reduce unnecessary escape of energy.

The door to the bathroom should generally stay shut!

290

If the bathroom is too small, there is a danger of energy stagnation. This can be prevented by hanging two mirrors opposite each other.

Plants not only feel comfortable in the bathroom because of the damp air, they also provide positive Qi.

Plants also lessen the volume of Qi flowing out through the toilet or other pipes, and inhibit stagnation of Qi.

291

If the dimensions of your home permit, create a toilet that is separate from the bathroom, or at least not directly visible. Where this is not possible, separate the toilet from the bathing area optically, and be sure the toilet cannot be seen from the door, not even in a mirror. The toilet should be as good as invisible in order to counteract the escape of Qi. The lid should always be closed (especially when flushing).

Remember—energy drainage represents disappearing wealth.

White, light blue or light green
are the best colours for bathrooms.

Natural light is preferable, but
where this is not possible, the room
should be well lit—not too brightly,
but reaching into every corner.

Immaculate cleanliness is the *non
plus ultra*.

293

Counterbalance the predominant Yang aspects of the bathroom with complementary Yin elements: ceramic, chrome or mirrors with hard, reflective surfaces (Yang) speed up Qi. Wooden accessories or small pieces of wood furniture, fluffy bath towels and bath mats create balancing Yin energy.

295

Whether you are longing for an invigorating shower or a relaxing bath, the bathroom can allow you to distance yourself from a hectic day. Relaxing bath oils, aromatic soaps or candles are wonderful aids.

陽

Burning incense or a few drops of essential oil in an oil-lamp in the bathroom can make daily stress disappear—try aromatic oils such as lavender, tangerine or sandalwood. A hot bath in the evenings is a good remedy if you are having trouble falling asleep.

296

297

Ceramic tiles on the bathroom floor are not only easy to clean, they also belong to the element Earth and thus balance the abundance of Water.

Car/Garage

Prosperity	Fame	Relation-ships
Family	Tai Ji Health	Children
Knowledge	Career	Patrons

The Ba-Gua scheme is even applicable to cars; the motor represents the entrance area. In front wheel drive vehicles, the life path and Career areas are over the hood. The passenger seat of rear wheel drive cars represents the Relationship area.

If you use your car frequently you should apply the most basic tenet of Feng Shui to it, as well: Clear away the rubbish in your car, and clean it frequently, inside and out!

299

Dents and scratches in your car
can have negative effects on the
corresponding areas of life.

300

301

The garage door should face north, and ideally the garage itself should stand detached from the house.

If this is not the case, the room next to the garage should be used as storage space.

Apartments

In apartments, all areas of life are united in a much smaller space. It is possible to apply the Ba-Gua scheme in such situations, but it is much more difficult to consider each area separately. Free space and peaceful zones are the most important priorities.

302

303

Order is the first commandment for one-room apartments.

Seating should never be placed so that people sit with their backs toward the window.

304

Lay the Ba-Gua figure over the floorplan of your apartment. According to the scheme, the centre of the room represents Health. The Career area lies in the north, Fame lies to the south, the area of Ancestors/Family is to the east, and Children are represented in the west, etc. Design your interior, as best you can, to promote all areas of life optimally.

In an apartment, the bathroom and kitchen are usually firmly installed, leaving little room for change. It is usually most productive to focus on the dining and sleeping areas.

306

307

Establish your sleeping area first,
and organise everything else around it.

308

Make sure that you do not have a direct view of the front door or the bathroom from your bed. Your feet should not be pointing toward them, either.

If these conditions cannot be avoided, use a screen to create a division.

309

Avoid allowing your bed to be "shut in" by walls or furniture on three sides.

310

If you cannot avoid placing a mirror near the bed, cover it with a cloth at night.

If you would like to create a work space, avoid having it too close to the bedroom, as this could inhibit your nights' rest. It is easier to integrate a work space into your living area than into the sleeping area.

311

In small spaces the dining table often serves a dual function as a desk. It thus makes sense to position this in the area of the apartment that corresponds to Prosperity.

Qi can be improved in small rooms by positioning plants, mobiles and mirrors. Carefully contemplate which areas you would like to improve, and then position objects accordingly to positively influence Qi.

313

Fish in the entrance to homes, shops and restaurants are seen as bearers of much good luck.

314

Symbolic representations of the luck-bearing animals dragons, tortoises or phoenixes are a must in the area corresponding to Fame. Emphasise the goals you have set for yourself by representing them, for example with a sporting trophy or other object.

315

316

Photos of your partner or a bouquet of fresh flowers in the area corresponding to Relationships can have a positive effect.

317

The Prosperity area is stimulated by the presence of water. Representations of water or fish are recommended.

318

It is a good idea to place photos of members of the family who are deceased in the Family/Ancestors area.

319

Pictures of mountains, an elephant or a tortoise are symbols that can enhance the area of Knowledge.

320

Images of stellar constellations, planned travel destinations, or clouds will positively affect the realm of Patrons.

321

A picture of a white tiger or pictures that have been painted by children are recommended in the Children's area.

322

Partnership

Beware of the Qi of your romantic predecessor! If your partner experienced a break-up in the apartment or house you are currently living in, you need to talk to your partner and then remove all traces of the predecessor! Check the space for unfavourable influences and change it so that you feel at home there.

323

All the influences that make daily life hectic have no business in your love nest, so no computer, no television, no bookshelves, etc. Children should also not be allowed into this area.

Make sure the temperature is pleasant, the air is fresh and the light complementary.

324

Problems with sex often derive from stress and a restricted energy flow. Allow yourself to relax, and take your mind off everyday life. Try breathing exercises or innovative love play.

325

326

Getting rid of trash and keeping order in a relationship means openness, the single most important factor for love to flow freely.

Express your wishes and your reservations. If you don't, inhibitions will surely develop.

327

A relationship feeds on attention, care and consideration. The same applies to flowers.

Place fresh flowers in the area corresponding to Relationships as a daily reminder that a partnership also requires tender loving care.

328

Terrace

A terrace creates a harmonious transition between the yard and the house, offering an additional opportunity to influence Qi.

The rules for the interior also apply here: Create space by cleaning up! The centre of the terrace should always remain clear, and even out of the way corners should never conceal garbage or clutter. Instead, liven them up with beautiful plants. Seating corners should be positioned along walls or borders.

329

The same is true for balconies—they should never become a permanent home for drying laundry or collections of old newspapers. Instead, positive Qi can be generated and spread to the entrance of your apartment by setting out just a few windowboxes or potted plants.

Climbing plants are an elegant way to conceal ugly exterior walls or walls with sharp edges. They also give us an extra portion of positive Qi.

If you plant flowering creepers, the scent and colour of their blossoms are an added bonus. Take care that the plants do not spread out over the entire surface, and mount a climbing support to prevent the tendrils from attaching their stubborn fine roots to the wall and damaging it due to collected moisture.

330

331

Garden

Feng Shiu strives to attain harmony and balance between opposing elements. This concept also applies to the garden. Low and high, light and dark, movement and stillness, hard and soft, rough and smooth properties should be combined.

332

From the perspective of Feng Shui, a rectangular or square garden is ideal. The entrance to the garden should be a well lit, curved path. Favourable objects include stone figures or large potted plants on both sides of the entrance. They will keep good luck on your property.

333

Hedges give your garden boundaries, hold on to Qi, occlude the neighbors' view into your yard, and offer animals a safe haven.

On the other hand, they should not grow so high that you lose contact with the surroundings or cannot see out.

334

Paths should be made of natural materials, gently curved and well secured. They should become narrower toward the house or entrance, and wider as they lead into the garden.

335

You should not be able to see all of the garden at once. Rather, your eyes should be guided from one area to the next as through a landscape.

336

Water collects energy and is the source of life for any garden. Create a small pond, waterfall or even a stream flowing through your garden.

But beware—water should not take up too much space in the garden design. Sometimes a bird-bath or fountain are enough. It is important that the water is always clean and clear.

Stationary bodies of water have a different effect than flowing water. A stream made too wide that flows away from the property will take energy with it, while a muddy pond affects Qi negatively. Splashing water in a fountain or waterfall can stimulate Qi. Think carefully about where and how you want to implement water!

337

338

Establish a niche for birds and other animals that includes hedges, bushes and a pond. Plants that attract butterflies, for instance, will enhance the life energy in your garden.

339

In yards with sufficient space, a small garden house or arbour can be a wonderful place to withdraw to. This spot should offer a good view of the garden.

340

Ideally, gardens should finish off with a hill, but a bountiful bush can serve this function, as well.

341

When choosing plants, keep in mind the ideal conditions for the plants in addition to the Feng Shui principles regarding location.

In cold climates the plants need to be winter resistant, for example. Plants that prefer shade should not be planted in direct sunlight or they will not thrive, even if their location is chosen favourably according to Feng Shui.

342

In China and Japan, gardens are places in which one can retreat from the strains of daily life. The Ba-Gua scheme can be an aid in creating a balanced design for your yard that allows you to target specific areas of your life for improvement.

The areas corresponding to Ancestors/Family and Prosperity are affiliated with the element Wood, and with sleight, pillar-shaped trees and bushes or climbing plants. The associated colours are green, blue, and shades of violet. The element Metal inhibits the flow of energy with its colours of silver, gold and white, while the colours of the element Water (black and dark shades of blue) are supportive. Some kind of seating is appropriate for the Ancestors/Family area, and a pond will boost Prosperity.

The area of Fame is dominated by the element Fire, the colours red, lilac and pink, and sharp plant leaves or thorns. Wood will stimulate this area if you introduce its colours—green and violet or light blue—or slim, pillar-like plants. The Fame area is an ideal location for a garden lamp or barbecue. Black or dark blue Water colours will inhibit this region.

344

345

Relationships, Knowledge and the Centre are affiliated with the element Earth. Accordingly, appropriate accessories are stone figures or terracotta pots. Plants growing along the floor or creepers with yellow and orange petals are well situated here. The stimulating element Fire can be introduced by planting red, pink or purple flowers or thorned plants. The inhibiting effects of Wood are achieved by using green, violet, light-blue or slim, pillar-like plants.

The Relationships area is a wonderful spot for an arbour or a small hut, offering a quiet retreat. The area corresponding to Knowledge should be protected from too much noise and excitement. Design it as an area of meditation where you can collect your thoughts and further your concentration. Because it is the focal point of your garden, which reflects your health, the Centre area should have a more open design.

347

The element Metal is affiliated with round plants, the colours gold, silver and white, and the areas of Children and Patrons. The element Earth (yellow and orange blossoms) will energise this area, while Fire (in the form of red or pink accents) is inhibiting. The Children's region is ideal for creating a play area, while a garden bench may be a more suitable tribute to the Patrons.

348

Water is the element corresponding to your Career. The colours dark blue or black are affiliated, as are plants with wavy leaves and an irregular profile. The element Metal is introduced by the presence of white, silver or gold and has a positive influence on this area, while everything connected to the element Earth is inhibiting. A fountain or bird-bath also lend momentum.

Since light and shade should be present in balanced proportions, you may want to plant a shaded garden in the shade of tall bushes or trees. Alyssum, ferns or decorative grasses are just a few of the plants you might include.

349

350

The Qi in a house surrounded by greenery can be positively affected, but take care that the windows are not "grown shut".

351

If your garden has a steep decline in it, Qi will flow away too quickly if you do not take measures to keep the energy in the garden. Stairs or heavy elements along the edges of a terrace can restrain the flow of Qi.

352

Too much of anything can be unhealthy. If you want to rejuvenate your garden with the addition of water or colour, keep in mind that excessive water can be damaging, just as too much colour can be unhealthy.

353

Animal Zodiac

Introduction

There are 12 animal zodiac signs: buffalo, rat, dragon, rabbit, tiger, snake, horse, monkey, rooster, goat, dog and pig.

Chinese astrology is based on the moon-cycle calendar, containing 60-year cycles. Each cycle is divided into 12 yearly divisions, according to the animal zodiac signs, and is related to the five elements.

Specific characteristics are allocated to each yearly division, thus also to each animal sign. The individual animal signs are also closely related to each other.

354

Buffalo

29/1/1949	through	16/2/1950
15/2/1961	through	4/2/1962
3/2/1973	through	22/1/1974
20/2/1985	through	8/2/1986
8/2/1997	through	27/2/1998
26/1/2009		

Characteristic for the year of the buffalo: hard work, exertion, discipline; less so creativity and new ideas.

The buffalo is intellectual, decisive and reliable.

The buffalo has positive associations with and positive phases in the year of the animal signs: snake and rooster.

Negative phases and associations in conjunction with: the goat

355

Rat

10/2/1948	through	28/1/1949
28/1/1960	through	14/2/1961
15/2/1972	through	2/2/1973
2/2/1984	through	19/2/1985
19/2/1996	through	6/2/1997
7/2/2008		

Characteristic for the year of the rat: long-term good business for all, solidity.

Positive associations with: rat, dragon, buffalo, goat, rooster, monkey

Negative associations with: dog, pig, horse

Dragon

27/1/1952	through	13/2/1953
13/2/1964	through	1/2/1965
31/1/1976	through	17/2/1977
17/2/1988	through	5/2/1989
5/2/2000	through	23/1/2001
23/1/2012		

The dragon years are attributed extraordinary characteristics: an unusual measure of success, initiative, energy, strength or power. If negative characteristics appear, these are also extreme, whether they are natural phenomena or personal changes.

Unreliability is also a characteristic of the dragon years.

Positive associations with: buffalo, dragon, snake, rooster, pig

Negative associations with: dog

357

Rabbit

6/2/1951	through	26/1/1952
25/1/1963	through	12/2/1964
11/2/1975	through	30/1/1976
29/1/1987	through	16/2/1988
16/2/1999	through	4/2/2000
3/2/2011		

Characteristic for the year of the rabbit: reliability, harmony and peace—and an absence of complications that can develop in a negative sense into indifference.

Those born in the sign of the rabbit have a good sense of humour, are easy-going and are willing to approach others; they are content people.

Positive associations with: dog, horse, goat, rabbit

Negative associations with: tiger, rooster, buffalo

358

Tiger

17/2/1950	through	5/2/1951
5/2/1962	through	24/1/1963
23/1/1974	through	10/2/1975
9/2/1986	through	28/2/1987
28/2/1998	through	15/2/1999
14/2/2010		

Characteristic for the year of the tiger: unreliability, conflict, threat, chaos, illness; private relations are ill-fated; the uncovering of irregularities.

Positive associations with: goat, rabbit, horse

Negative associations with: dragon, buffalo, rat, monkey

359

Snake

14/2/1953	through	2/2/1954
2/2/1965	through	20/1/1966
18/2/1977	through	6/2/1978
6/2/1989	through	26/1/1990
24/1/2001	through	11/2/2002
10/2/2013		

Characteristic for the year of the snake: style, aesthetic sense, calmness, artistic development

Tensions are not mentioned, but could nevertheless exist.

Positive associations with: dog, pig, monkey, rooster, rabbit

Negative associations with: dragon, tiger

360

Horse

3/2/1954	through	23/1/1955
21/1/1966	through	8/2/1967
7/2/1978	through	27/1/1979
27/1/1990	through	14/2/1991
12/2/2002	through	31/1/2003
31/1/2014		

Characteristic for the year of the horse: the realisation of plans, grasping of initiative, development of ideas, a view toward the future. Difficult tasks are undertaken with utmost self-confidence.

People born in the year of the horse are active, open and popular, people of action.

Positive associations with: monkey, dog, horse, rabbit

Negative associations with: rat, pig

361

Monkey

12/2/1956	through	30/1/1957
30/1/1968	through	16/2/1969
16/2/1980	through	4/2/1981
4/2/1992	through	22/1/1993
22/1/2004	through	8/2/2005
8/2/2016		

Characteristic for the year of the monkey: creative joy, willingness to take risks, intelligence and aptitude, activity; large business transactions will be undertaken.

Those born under the sign of the monkey are clever, self-confident and creative; they are active personalities.

Positive associations with: rat, rabbit, rooster, monkey, dragon

Negative associations with: tiger, dog, pig

362

Rooster

31/1/1957	through	17/2/1958
17/2/1969	through	5/2/1970
5/2/1981	through	24/1/1982
23/1/1993	through	9/2/1994
9/2/2005	through	28/2/2006
28/1/2017		

Characteristic for the year of the rooster: rebellion without decisive developments; nevertheless, stability in economic matters.

Roosters are thought to be proud—they puff up their chests and cannot tolerate criticism.

Positive associations with: rooster, dog, snake, goat, tiger, dragon

Negative associations with: rat, horse

363

Goat

24/1/1955	through	11/2/1956
9/2/1967	through	29/1/1968
28/1/1979	through	15/2/1980
15/2/1991	through	3/2/1992
1/2/2003	through	21/1/2004
19/2/2015		

Characteristic for the year of the goat: calm, a harmonious family life, a tendency to be reserved, leisure activities are at the forefront.

Those born under the sign of the goat are tolerate, honest, sensitive, indulgent and understanding.

Positive associations with: horse, monkey, rooster, rat, snake

Negative associations with: goat, dog, buffalo

Dog

18/2/1958	through	7/2/1959
6/2/1970	through	26/1/1971
25/1/1982	through	12/2/1983
10/2/1994	through	30/1/1995
29/2/2006	through	17/1/2007
16/2/2018		

Characteristic for the year of the dog: balance—there are no particularly positive or negative events, and therefore also no great expectations; harmony must be created anew over and over again.

People born in the year of the dog are loyal and honest, stubborn and decisive, if a little prone to worrying, and not inclined to experiment.

Positive associations with: rat, horse, snake, dog

Negative associations with: rooster, dragon

365

Pig

8/2/1959	through	27/1/1960
27/1/1971	through	15/1/1972
13/2/1983	through	1/2/1984
31/1/1995	through	18/2/1996
18/2/2007	through	6/2/2008
5/2/2019		

Characteristic for the year of the pig: joie de vivre, opulence, happy developments and profits, but also addiction to pleasure and wastefulness.

Those born under the sign of the pig are superficial, generous and friendly, but tend to be decadent.

Positive associations with: dragon, buffalo, horse

Negative associations with: tiger, dog, rat

The Chinese astrological calendar:

Year	(New Year)	Zodiac Sign	Element
1928	(23.1.)	dragon	Earth
1929	(10.2.)	snake	Earth
1930	(30.1.)	horse	Metal
1931	(17.2.)	sheep	Metal
1932	(6.2.)	monkey	Water
1933	(26.1.)	rooster	Water
1934	(14.2.)	dog	Wood
1935	(4.2.)	pig	Wood
1936	(24.1.)	rat	Fire
1937	(11.2.)	ox	Fire
1938	(31.1.)	tiger	Earth
1939	(19.2.)	rabbit	Earth
1940	(8.2.)	dragon	Metal
1941	(27.1.)	snake	Metal
1942	(15.2.)	horse	Water
1943	(5.2.)	sheep	Water
1944	(25.1.)	monkey	Wood
1945	(13.2.)	rooster	Wood
1946	(2.2.)	dog	Fire
1947	(22.1.)	pig	Fire
1948	(10.2.)	rat	Earth
1949	(29.1.)	ox	Earth
1950	(17.2.)	tiger	Metal
1951	(6.2.)	rabbit	Metal
1952	(27.1.)	dragon	Water
1953	(14.2.)	snake	Water

1954	(3.2.)	horse	Wood
1955	(24.1.)	sheep	Wood
1956	(12.2.)	monkey	Fire
1957	(31.1.)	rooster	Fire
1958	(18.2.)	dog	Earth
1959	(8.2.)	pig	Earth
1960	(28.1.)	rat	Metal
1961	(15.2.)	ox	Metal
1962	(5.2.)	tiger	Water
1963	(25.1.)	rabbit	Water
1964	(13.2.)	dragon	Wood
1965	(2.2.)	snake	Wood
1966	(21.1.)	horse	Fire
1967	(9.2.)	sheep	Fire
1968	(31.1.)	monkey	Earth
1969	(17.2.)	rooster	Earth
1970	(6.2.)	dog	Metal
1971	(27.1.)	pig	Metal
1972	(15.2.)	rat	Water
1973	(3.2.)	ox	Water
1974	(23.1.)	tiger	Wood
1975	(11.2.)	rabbit	Wood
1976	(31.1.)	dragon	Fire
1977	(18.2.)	snake	Fire
1978	(7.2.)	horse	Earth
1979	(28.1.)	sheep	Earth
1980	(16.2.)	monkey	Metal